THE TWO OLD MEN

The Two Old Men

What Makes Them Differ?

BY REV.

CAESAR MALAN

OF GENEVA

CURIOSMITH

MINNEAPOLIS

Published by Curiosmith.
Minneapolis, Minnesota.
Internet: curiosmith.com.

Previously published by THE RELIGIOUS TRACT
SOCIETY in 1819.

ISBN 9781941281949

CONTENTS

The Two Old Men . . . 7

About the Author . . . 45

About this Book . . . 47

Man's Questions and God's Answers . . . 48

The Two Old Men

What Makes Them Differ?

I had occasion to visit a distant part of my parish—the afternoon was fine, and I chose a path which presented varied and extensive prospects. As I ascended an eminence, I saw an aged laborer before me, who proceeded slowly along, bending under a heavy burden of wood. I knew something of this man—he was generally respected among his neighbors, and was spoken of as an example for regular attendance on public worship, and for general integrity of conduct.

As I came near, I heard him

complaining to himself.

"Hard fate," said he; "how many troubles fall to my lot. At seventy years old I am obliged to work from morning till night; and, after all, can hardly keep myself from starving. But so it is, and it is of no use to complain."

As he spoke these words, he laid down his burden, and stopped to rest.

"You seem tired, my friend," said I. "The path is steep and rough, and you are not so strong as you used to be."

OLD MAN. It is the case with all, sir, as they grow old.

MINISTER. If the old man has learned wisdom, he will find comfort in reflecting that his labor is nearly over.

OLD MAN. What you say is true, sir; we must soon go hence; but it is hard to have had nothing but trouble here. Well, let it pass; I am almost at the end of my journey.

MINISTER. Happy are those who, while journeying here, are enabled to look to the Savior. Old age has no terrors for them.

OLD MAN. You are right, sir; but religion does not prevent our meeting with troubles. I am a proof of this, sir; no one can be more religious than I have been: I go regularly to church, and I never worked on Sundays; and, thank God, I can say, without boasting, that I am an honest man; but, after all, no one has met with more misfortunes than I have.

MINISTER. Doubtless, you have had your trials; but, my friend, are you right in calling them misfortunes? God sends afflictions for our good.

OLD MAN. I have nothing to say against it, sir; but when I look around me, and see so many wicked—I do

HAPPY ARE THOSE WHO, WHILE JOURNEYING HERE, ARE ENABLED TO LOOK TO THE SAVIOR.

not wish to speak ill of my neighbors—thank God, I am not guilty of that sin; but every body knows, that there are people who drink, and swear, and go neither to church nor meeting, and never trouble themselves about another world, and yet they live quite at their ease, and have every thing comfortable about them. Now, sir, I will freely own, that when I see these things, I cannot help asking myself, whether it was worth my while to take all this trouble to be religious; for what have I got by it? My two sons have cost me money without end; and, after all, it was of no use, for they died: and my wife's last illness took what little I had left; and here am I, turned of seventy, without a shilling in the world, and obliged to work as a day-laborer. Surely, my lot is a hard one!

Minister. I am very sorry to hear you speak in this manner. I thought that you had been a Christian, but I see no proof of it.

Old Man. I beg your pardon, sir. Thank God, I am a Christian; and I have no doubt I shall go to heaven when I die.

Minister. Tell me; how do you expect to get there?

OLD MAN. The same way as others, to be sure. I am an honest man; I have done nobody any harm; and, though I may not always have been quite so good as I ought, I am not worse than my neighbors; and after all, God is merciful, and he will pardon those who repent, and are sorry for what they have done wrong.

MINISTER. You are right, my friend, in saying that God is merciful; but you should remember he is just also, and that we have all sinned against him, and there is no forgiveness, except through Christ Jesus.

OLD MAN. Who denies this, sir? We must be Christians, or we cannot go to heaven.

MINISTER. What is being a Christian?

OLD MAN. As to that, sir, every body best knows his own meaning.

For my part, I am not one of those who think they see more in religion than their neighbors. If I do my best, it is all that is required of me, and I believe in God, and in Jesus Christ, and give myself no trouble as to any thing further.

MINISTER. But, my good friend, are you certain that you believe in Jesus Christ? Perhaps you may be mistaken as to this.

OLD MAN. Sir, I am very sure that a good man will do what his conscience tells him he ought to do; and if he does this, God will not condemn him for not having believed what he did not understand.

MINISTER. But supposing he has neglected what he did know? And I cannot help saying to you, Take care; for much is required of you, and your time is now short.

OLD MAN. Thank you, sir, for your advice; but I hope to live some years longer. I do not think my time will come just yet.

MINISTER. Ah, my friend, if you knew the Savior, you would be ready to depart hence, and to be with him, instead of wishing to continue in this world.

OLD MAN. All in good time, sir: while we are here; let us make the best of this world; when we are in heaven, we shall have time enough to think of these things.

MINISTER. My poor old man! Is this all your hope? With eternity before you, upon the point of being summoned to appear before your God, you have no trust except in your own righteousness. You boast that you have not been a thief, or a murderer, or a slanderer, but you know not the sinfulness of your heart, and you are ignorant of the way of salvation, through faith in Christ Jesus. My good friend, I must tell you that your soul is in great danger.

OLD MAN. I hope not, sir; I hope not. I have no fear about the matter. I do my duty—I go to church—I say my prayers—I read the Bible now and then—this is more than most people do; and, no doubt, I shall get safe to heaven at last.

MINISTER. My friend, I fear much for you, and I must speak to you again about these things; think more about them. I will call upon you in a day or two; I cannot now stop any longer.

OLD MAN. I shall be glad to see you, sir; I like to talk about religion. Good day, sir.

Fervently I implored Him "that openeth, and no man shutteth,"[1] to

1 Revelation 3:7.

have compassion upon this poor sinner, and to enable me to speak a word in season the next time I saw him. "This, then," said I, as I proceeded on my way, "is the religion with which man decks himself before his fellow-mortals! By this hardness of heart, and this self-confidence, he has acquired that reputation of which he is so vain! A few accustomed phrases, decency in his outward conduct, and a constant readiness to blame the faults of others, may be enough to satisfy those who only regard outward appearances; 'But the Lord looketh on the heart.'[1] What hope, then, is there for his soul? What is the ground of his confidence before that just and holy God, since he desires not the knowledge of the Lord; still less does he seek to be reconciled to God, by fleeing for refuge to the

1   1 Samuel 16:7.

hope set before him in Jesus Christ, the only and beloved Son of God, who alone is the way, the truth, and the life? Who has this man chosen for his Savior? Alas! he does not even feel his need of one. Dreadful ignorance! 'When they shall say, peace and safety, then sudden destruction cometh upon them.'[1] An aged person, still ignorant of our Savior, is indeed to be pitied! Is there ground to hope that he will awaken from this spiritual slumber before the sleep of death overtake him; and what is this first death now at hand, when compared with that which *must* come, and which is emphatically called 'the second death?'[2] Surely, then, it is peculiarly the duty of all, who are the children of God, to pray earnestly and at all times, that he would have

1   1 Thessalonians 5:3.
2   Revelation 20:14.

compassion upon the aged, who yet remain ignorant of his salvation, and awaken them, while it is yet time, while it is yet called today."

My mind was still engaged in these important reflections, when I arrived at the first of the cottages I came to visit. It was a humble dwelling, built against a rock which rose abruptly from the side of a hill; embosomed in trees, which covered it with their luxuriant foliage; at a small distance was an orchard; a rivulet, rising from a higher part of the hill, flowed past the cottage, and was lost in plantations of osier.

Here dwelt one of the most aged of my parishioners, generally known by the name of Old William. He had built upon a rock, not as to his earthly dwelling only; his hopes for eternity rested upon the *Rock of ages*. These hopes filled him with peace and joy in believing; and had supported him under the privations and infirmities of age. His lot had been one of trial and suffering; for, after having lived happily for many years, with a wife whom he dearly loved, he had followed her to the grave; and had also lost, in early life, three promising children; while two others, who had survived, were removed to a distance, and he had now no one to live with him except one of his grandchildren and an aged laborer.

I often called upon this old man, and always found that I was benefited by his conversation. His religion was calm and simple, and free from guile; the words he uttered spoke the inward peace which possessed his soul. Whenever he mentioned his past trials and sufferings, he dwelt so much upon the love of his Savior, that it was impossible not to feel affected by that influence which ever accompanies true faith, and which gives a foretaste of joys to come. As I drew near the house, I saw the old man sitting at the door, and his grandson standing between his knees. The old man was speaking earnestly; and they were too much engaged to observe my approach.

"No, my child," said he, "we sorrow not for your father, as without hope: his body, it is true, lies in the grave, but his soul is with Him who loved and redeemed him. Do you remember your father? Oh! may you be a disciple of Christ, as he was. Shall not I soon be with him?"

"And shall not I go too?" said the boy.

"I hope you will, my child: God is the father of the fatherless; trust in him, I must soon leave you."

At these words the child burst into tears. I called him to me, and said what I could to comfort him, and, taking a little book from my pocket, "Go, my dear," said I, "sit down under that tree, and read this; you will find it tells you that God will never forget his children."

"My friend," said I, as soon as I was alone with the old man, "let us bless the Lord at all times, and under all the dispensations of his providence."

OLD WILLIAM. Yes, for he is our Father; he is always kind to us. "Like as a father pitieth his children, so the Lord pitieth them that fear him."[1]

MINISTER. I rejoice, my brother, to find, that, in your old age, you are thus supported by the Lord; and that your faith is strengthened as the hour of your departure draws nigh. Your lot

1   Psalm 103:13.

appears to me desirable.

OLD WILLIAM. Sir, I have indeed much cause for rejoicing—the Lord crowns me with his loving-kindness.

MINISTER. Your past troubles, and the recollection of them, are no longer too bitter for you to bear; the sufferings of old age are not beyond your strength to sustain.

OLD WILLIAM. Ah, sir, you know better than I do from whence our strength is derived. The Lord has said, "My grace is sufficient for thee; for my strength is made perfect in weakness."[1] I did not always think so: some events in my past life have troubled and cast me down, and more than once did I forget Him in whom alone we have strength, and then I gave way to unbelief. I recollect, particularly, one of these bitter trials, which I was ready to

1   2 Corinthians 12:9.

sink under; but the Savior remembered his promise, though I had forgotten it. He would not let me go, though I was ready to depart from him. I had just lost my dear wife; she left this world rejoicing and trusting in Him who loved and redeemed her; and, like the martyr Stephen, she appeared to have a glimpse of the glory of her Redeemer, even in this world of sin and suffering; yet my hard, unthankful heart praised him not for this loving-kindness towards her; I felt stunned and angered under my loss; I submitted, it is true, but I submitted not willingly; I did not say, "It is the Lord, let him do what seemeth him good."[1] But God loves us with real love, and draws towards him the heart which is not of itself inclined to seek him, and according to his word I have found, that "whom

1   1 Samuel 3:18.

the Lord loveth, he chasteneth."[1] I had been one day to a neighboring village, to plant some flowers on the grave of my dear wife. On my return, I saw a thick smoke rising from the ruins of my barn—it was consumed, and all my little harvest—all that I had stored up for my family. Thou, O Lord, hast pardoned me; but thou knowest that the first thoughts of that hard heart, which is still within me, were to murmur and complain. I was ready to say, "What doest thou?"[2] I entered my cottage, and there a more dreadful scene met my eyes; I saw Daniel, my eldest son, the comfort and stay of my age the support of my family, and an example to all who knew him, lying on the floor, scorched, burnt, and disfigured, while some friends were

1 Hebrews 12:6.
2 Job 9:12.

applying remedies; but the injuries he had received were too severe, and he soon afterwards expired. He had rushed into the middle of the flames, and saved his youngest sister, but God was pleased to call him hence by this his work and labor of love. Never can I recollect that day without bitterness of soul; and that, not so much from the remembrance of this affliction, severe as it was, but from calling to mind my unbelief, and murmuring against thee, O Lord. Would you believe, sir, that my Daniel, full of faith and rejoicing, even under the painful agonies he then suffered, should be able to comfort, or, I would rather say, to shame his wretched father?

"I can no longer see you, my father," said he, "but I hear what you say, and it grieves me. O, my father, you are complaining against God."

"It is more," cried I, "than I can bear."

"Yes, my father, it is more than you can bear, but it is the Lord's doing; he has sent you this trial; and as for me, I am about to depart hence, and be with him for ever."

"But why could he not spare you a few years longer?"

My son replied not, but in a low voice he prayed, "Come, Lord Jesus; O! come quickly." Then asking for his wife and their infant, he commended them to Him who feeds the fowls of the air, and clothes the grass of the field.[1] "Elizabeth," added he, "remember that your husband is going to be with Christ, and teach our Benjamin that there is a Savior."

These were his last words. Since that time she has joined him above.

1   Matthew 6:26–34.

But I murmured against thee, O Lord, and cried, "Wherefore is light given to him that is in misery, and life unto the bitter in soul?"[1]

MINISTER. Your mind now is at peace, and you have experienced that, although "no chastening for the present seemeth to be joyous, but grievous; nevertheless, afterward it yieldeth the peaceable fruit of righteousness unto them which are exercised thereby."[2]

OLD WILLIAM. Yes, sir, I am now enabled to say, "It is good for me that I have been afflicted."[3] I perceive how great has been the mercy of the Lord to my soul; I now can see the way by which he has led me, and which I knew not; it is far better than the way I desired to choose myself. The Lord

1   Job 3:20.
2   Hebrews 12:11.
3   Psalm 119:71.

seemed to visit me in his displeasure: these dispensations, to worldly eyes, appeared the effects of divine wrath; but I know that they are the remedies which are needful for the healing of my soul. Yes, my Savior, thou art full of compassion and loving-kindness towards me, wretched sinner that I am.

Minister. Ere long, my friend, you will be with Him who has "loved thee with an everlasting love,"[1] and "who was delivered for our offenses."[2]

"Yes; may it be soon," said the old man, raising his eyes towards heaven, with an expression of love and joy which I cannot describe, and which surpassed any thing have ever seen in others.

I have often marked the peace and serenity which appeared upon the

1   Jeremiah 31:3.
2   Romans 4:25.

countenances of aged persons, who knew the Savior, and trusted in him alone—far different from the anxious, careworn expression of those who have grown old in the love of the world, and the things which are in it; but I never before so strongly marked that divine seal of the hope which "maketh not ashamed."[1] It is true, that I, perhaps, never before found a heart so sincerely attached to Christ, nor a Christian who felt so deeply that he was a stranger and pilgrim on the earth,[2] hastening towards that "house not made with hands, eternal in the heavens."[3]

I think that aged pilgrims frequently fall short of their privileges. They are in general deeply anxious respecting the salvation of their souls;

---

1   Romans 5:5.

2   Hebrews 11:13.

3   2 Corinthians 5:1.

for how is it possible to be uncon-
cerned, when they cannot but feel
that eternity is just at hand!—when
the infirmities of a body, worn out by
sin and worldly cares, remind them
at every step, that they must soon
be laid in that narrow house which
is appointed for all living, there to
return, earth to earth, and ashes to
ashes! The old man, now arrived at
that age which is the term appointed
for the life of the children of men, if he
does not suffer himself to be blinded
by the vain imaginations of his own
heart, and the false, flattering hopes
of his friends, must daily feel, "I have
run my appointed course: I must soon
depart hence, and that for ever." Then,
unless he is willing his soul should be
lost for ever, surely he will look to
Jesus. "For there is none other name
under heaven, given among men,

whereby we must be saved."[1] Yet, how seldom do we find, beneath gray hairs, a "desire to depart, and to be with Christ."[2] Few indeed are there, who are found looking for, and anxiously waiting the coming of that day, when they shall enter upon another and a better world. Still fewer are there, who, like this old man, have cast themselves entirely upon the Savior and his finished redemption. Happy is the soul who can thus contemplate the Savior dying for us men, and for our salvation; the remembrance of past transgressions at once humbles him in the dust before his Lord, and excites his admiration for the "great love wherewith he loved us."[3]

OLD WILLIAM. This, sir, is the

---

1   Acts 4:12.
2   Philippians 1:23.
3   Ephesians 2:4.

ground of my hope and rejoicing,
when I think of the world to come.
When I sit here, at evening, while
Benjamin is collecting his sheep, I
call to mind the days of my pilgrim-
age, fewer in number and more evil
than those of Jacob,[1] and how far
does the long-suffering and the love
of God appear to pass human under-
standing—I seem lost, when I reflect
thereon. I recollect the time when
I built this little cottage: I was just
turned of thirty, and about to marry.
I had lived, as most of our country-
men do, without seriously thinking
of the concerns of my soul, and only
a few occasional thoughts upon the
subject had passed across my mind. I
felt, however, desirous to pursue these
thoughts. How kind was the Savior
towards me! It was indeed by bands

1   Genesis 47:9.

of love,[1] that he drew me to him. He united me to one of his children—my dear Susan was a follower of Christ— she was the only daughter of a poor widow, who lived at that white cottage which you see at the end of the valley. How often have we walked by the side of that little stream, conversing about these things. She was always the first to begin this subject; and she, by divine grace, was the means appointed to teach me that I was a poor sinner, but that Christ died for me.

MINISTER. The Lord blessed you in thus granting, what, according to his word, is a favor from him.[2]

OLD WILLIAM. She was indeed a blessing from him, and therefore I ought to have given him all my heart, and to have lived only to him, as

1   Hosea 11:4.
2   Proverbs 18:22.

she lived. But how often have I grieved her by the hardness of my heart towards God. Often has she said to me, "O! why will not you love the Savior? The pride of your heart will not allow you to accept the salvation he offers, because it is 'without money, and without price,'[1] but rest assured that it is more certain and more sweet to receive this as a free gift from our God, than to harass and torment yourself as you do, with the vain hope of being able to work out salvation for yourself."

Minister. You were then righteous in your own eyes, and forgot, that of yourself you had no power to do good works, pleasant and acceptable to God; but supposed that your own good deeds would blot out your sins, and ransom your soul from condemnation.

1   Isaiah 55:1.

OLD WILLIAM. It is true, sir, I felt a secret repugnance and dislike to the great and consoling truth, that "a sinner can only be justified before God, by the righteousness and the blood of Christ." I loathed the idea of "being justified freely by his grace, through the redemption that is in Christ Jesus."[1] To relinquish my own righteousness, and seek to be clothed with his righteousness; to renounce all that I had secretly prided myself upon, and relinquish all that I had done in my own strength—in short, that "all our righteousnesses are as filthy rags" in the sight of God, was hateful to me.[2] These doctrines of the Gospel hurt the pride of my heart. I strove with my Maker, and felt angry with my patient and affectionate wife, who, seeing me thus refusing the

---

1   Romans 3:24.
2   Isaiah 64:6.

offer of salvation through the blood of Christ, disputed not with me, but continued to point out the Savior to me as "the Lamb of God, which taketh away the sin of the world."[1] But now mercy has been extended to me, "My soul shall be joyful in my God, for he hath clothed me with the garments of salvation; he hath covered me with the robe of righteousness."[2]

MINISTER. But do you not still "groan, being burdened" with sin and suffering; do not your daily offenses against God cause you much grief and bitterness of soul?

OLD WILLIAM. Yes, daily do I long for that happy moment when my soul shall be freed from sin; when I shall be called to depart hence, and to be with Christ. The accomplishment of this

1 John 1:29.
2 Isaiah 61:10.

hope appears now at hand, and this alone supports and sustains me. Oh, sir, you know not how I wish to be freed from the power of unbelief; how I groan, being burdened by this body of sin and death.

MINISTER. Then are you not yet at peace with God?

OLD WILLIAM. Thanks be to God, sir, for the inestimable gift; he has not left me in doubt of his love towards me. I know that it is an unchanging love; and that the love, wherewith he loved me, while yet his enemy,[1] will not be taken away, seeing that I am now justified by his blood,[2] and, to use the words of the apostle, "I am persuaded that neither death, nor life, nor angels, nor principalities, nor powers, nor things present, nor things

1 Romans 5:10.
2 Romans 5:9.

to come, nor height, nor depth, nor any other creature, shall be able to separate us from the love of God, which is in Christ Jesus our Lord,"[1] which he has testified unto me, "according to the good pleasure of his will."[2] I often think that I act towards my heavenly Father somewhat in the manner in which my little Benjamin acts towards me, if I may make such a comparison. The child knows that I love him, and he desires to please me; but sometimes, forgetting my affection and his duty, he does something displeasing to me; but the poor child does not, therefore, doubt that I am his "dear father," as he calls me; and I do not forget that he is "my child"; but I hasten to turn his heart towards me, that he may find peace and comfort.

1   Romans 8:38, 39.
2   Ephesians 1:5.

Benjamin can easily count the times that I forgive him, but how can I number the loving-kindnesses of the Lord towards me; have I not sufficient ground to rest myself upon the mercy and loving-kindness of Him who says, "Fear not, for I have redeemed thee?"[1]

MINISTER. Happy old man! Happy believer in Christ! You seem already to enjoy a foretaste of that happiness which is to come.

OLD WILLIAM. Oh, sir, speak to me only of the mercy and loving-kindness of my Savior—that is what my soul requires, and thirsts to hear. Tell me that the treasures of his grace and long-suffering are inexhaustible—that is the ground of my confidence. Tell me, again and again, that salvation is by Christ alone, so that I may more and more desire to

1   Isaiah 43:1.

be "found in him."[1] Show him to me "meek and lowly in heart,"[2] the friend of sinners,[3] "the Lamb that was slain" for me.[4] Show me these things, that I may not dread the day when "he shall come to judge the world." Tell me, tell me that Christ died for me, and that is all I wish, all that I can require.

MINISTER. Christ himself tells you this. By his Holy Spirit he has revealed it to you; and he will increase this assurance every day and every hour that you remain in this world. Rejoice, then, happy old man, because your name is written in the book of life.[5] Yet a little while, a few days more, and you will be removed to the place prepared for you

---

1   Philippians 3:9.
2   Matthew 11:29.
3   Matthew 11:19.
4   Revelation 5:12.
5   Philippians 4:3; Luke 10:20.

in your "Father's house,"[1] and the love of Christ shall be your life eternal.

"May these things be so," said the old man.

"I must now leave you," said I, "but I rejoice, with the truest joy which a minister of Christ can possess, that there is at least one of my flock, who will quit this world of sorrow to enter into eternal happiness."

———————————

My reader, reflect a little upon this narrative, especially if you are advanced in life.

You have heard the sentiments of two men, two of your fellow-mortals, whose hour of death was at hand, and whose souls, like yours, will never die. It is not a matter of choice with us; but whether we desire it or not, our souls <u>must appear</u> before the judgment-seat

1   John 14:2, 3.

of Christ. These two men were each of them desirous that their souls should enjoy happiness in the world to come, and each of them thought that he had found the path that leadeth to life eternal. But which of them was right? Ask yourself, my reader; ask your conscience, for it is certain that there is only one way by which we can obtain eternal happiness, and you must have seen that these two men pursued different paths.

Was that man right, who, trusting in his fancied good works, and full of his own righteousness, had the name of Jesus on his lips only, and not in his heart; who imagined that every one who called himself a Christian was, in reality, a follower of Christ?

Or do you think him right—that pious and humble man—who had placed his foundation on "the Rock of ages!" who ascribed all the glory of his salvation to the Savior; and who trusted only in his blood, shed for us upon the cross?

Surely you cannot doubt on this subject. Your own heart will tell you that the latter was the Christian, and that he had the faith which saveth.

Haste, then, my aged friend, haste, while there is yet time. "Now is the accepted time—now is the day of salvation,"[1] but it is fast fleeing away, you are now at the "eleventh hour"; hasten and cast yourself upon the Lord; give your heart to Him who alone can save; and rest your hopes of salvation on Christ alone, and not upon yourself. May he be pleased to hear you; and may he, by his Holy Spirit, enable you to come unto him, who has declared, that to those who

1   2 Corinthians 6:2.

ask, it shall be given; that those who seek shall find.[1]

Let the humble Christian, who is mourning because he is not able to feel confident and assured of his interest in Christ, not be discouraged and cast down; but let the sense of his weakness and unbelief drive him to the throne of grace, and make him willing to derive grace and strength from that fullness which is treasured up in Christ Jesus. Let him remember that he may do this. The words of the apostle are, "casting all your care upon Him, for he careth for you."[2] "All are yours, and ye are Christ's, and Christ is God's."[3]

---

1   Matthew 7:7.
2   1 Peter 5:7.
3   1 Corinthians 3:22, 23.

About the Author

Henri Abraham Caesar Malan (1787–1864), was born in Geneva, Switzerland and educated at Geneva College. He was ordained into ministry in 1810. He married the following year. But it wasn't until 1814 that he received the truth of Jesus Christ, the message that he had been preaching. Henri preached against formalism of the church and spiritual apathy. In 1820 he built his own chapel to be separate from the National Church of Geneva. He received the Doctor of Divinity from the University of Glasgow in 1826. Besides books and tracts, he wrote hymns, both words and music. He was the father of Solomon Caesar Malan, an accomplished linguist.

About this Book

THE TWO CONVERSATIONS are of men with different characters. The first one, called Old Man, was confident of being a Christian and going to heaven, because he was generally a good person. The second man called Old William, was convinced of his corrupt nature and so trusted in Christ for his salvation, but was plagued by thoughts of past unworthiness. "Happy are those who, while journeying here, are enabled to look to the Savior. Old age has no terrors for them."

The ATS description: The author's conversations, in the form of dialogue, with two aged men; the first a lukewarm formalist, trusting in his own fancied good works; the other a humble evangelical disciple of Christ: presenting the two characters in contrast.

Man's Questions & God's Answers

Am I accountable to God?
Each of us will give an account of himself to God.
ROMANS 14:12 (NIV).

Has God seen all my ways?
Everything is uncovered and laid bare before the eyes of him to whom we must give account.
HEBREWS 4:13 (NIV).

Does he charge me with sin?
But the Scripture declares that the whole world is a prisoner of sin. GALATIANS 3:22 (NIV).
All have sinned and fall short of the glory of God.
ROMANS 3:23 (NIV).

Will he punish sin?
The soul who sins is the one who will die.
EZEKIEL 18:4 (NIV).
For the wages of sin is death, but the gift of God is eternal life in Christ Jesus our Lord.
ROMANS 6:23 (NIV).

Must I perish?
He is patient with you, not wanting anyone to perish, but everyone to come to repentance.
2 PETER 3:9 (NIV).

How can I escape?
Believe in the Lord Jesus, and you will be saved.
ACTS 16:31 (NIV).

Is he able to save me?

Therefore he is able to save completely those who come to God through him. HEBREWS 7:25 (NIV).

Is he willing?

Christ Jesus came into the world to save sinners. 1 TIMOTHY 1:15 (NIV).

Am I saved on believing?

Whoever believes in the Son has eternal life, but whoever rejects the Son will not see life, for God's wrath remains on him. JOHN 3:36 (NIV).

Can I be saved now?

Now is the time of God's favor, now is the day of salvation. 2 CORINTHIANS 6:2 (NIV).

As I am?

Whoever comes to me I will never drive away. JOHN 6:37 (NIV).

Shall I not fall away?

Him who is able to keep you from falling. JUDE 1:24 (NIV).

If saved, how should I live?

Those who live should no longer live for themselves but for him who died for them and was raised again. 2 CORINTHIANS 5:15 (NIV).

What about death and eternity?

I am going there to prepare a place for you. I will come back and take you to be with me that you also may be where I am. JOHN 14:2-3 (NIV).

Printed in Great Britain
by Amazon

61498108R00031